Wildshots

The World of the Wildlife Photographer

NATHAN AASENG

The Millbrook Press, Brookfield, Connecticut

CONTENTS

CHAPTER 1

Hunting With a Camera

Joe McDonald knew from the instant he broke out of the forest and into the clearing that he had struck gold. The professional wildlife photographer spent thirty weeks a year conducting photographic tours and workshops and much of the rest of the year prowling the woods and wilderness for appealing subjects to photograph. The more time he lingered in the stillness of nature, the more his appreciation of wildlife and the fragile beauty of nature had grown. But he had never seen anything that took his breath away like the magical scene before him.

Wildlife photographer Joe McDonald knew he had struck gold when he came upon a group of bull elk feeding in the early morning light in the Western Rockies. This photo is one of that series.

"Suddenly we came to a knoll overlooking one of the greatest wildlife spectacles on Earth." In the middle of a thundering waterfall, **sixteen huge Alaskan brown bears** were feeding on the salmon that swam upstream to their spawning grounds.

McDonald had arrived at a thermal spring at just the right time to see four bull elk feeding at the pool. The rich dawn light combined with the thick, steamy mist of the warm water vapor clashing with the early morning cold air to create an eerie, mystical backdrop for these beautiful animals. McDonald was overwhelmed by the "scene's moody quality. Mist rising from the pond first enveloped the elk and then gradually parted to reveal their outlines."

As a wildlife photographer, McDonald was doubly privileged. Not only could he personally savor such a rare scene but he could use his expertise and experience to capture the moment on film so that hundreds of thousands of people could share in the experience.

Wildlife photographers Erwin and Peggy Bauer, who have traveled to many of the most remote and exotic places in the world during their celebrated careers, know the feeling. After flying in by airplane to a remote camp along the McNeil River in the Alaska Peninsula, they hiked for an hour across lagoons and up a steep bluff. Seeing bear tracks and hearing snorts in the high grass, they shouted to warn the bears of their presence.

In the Bauers' words, "Suddenly we came to a knoll overlooking one of the greatest wildlife spectacles on Earth." In the middle of a thundering waterfall, sixteen huge Alaskan brown bears were feeding on the salmon that swam upstream to their spawning grounds. Arriving and leaving on trails followed by their ancestors for hundreds of years, bears of all ages fought for choice positions in the churning river. With varying degrees of skills, they stalked the fish and slapped them out of the water.

The Bauers' photography expeditions have rewarded them with many awe-inspiring moments such as a brief but violent clash between two bull elk in rutting season to a stare down with a rarely seen tiger lingering near a kill in India. Yet no matter how many of nature's wonders they experienced, their appreciation continued to grow. "Even during a lifetime of hunting with a camera," they wrote of the Alaskan bear experience, "it is an extraordinary scene."

A Glamorous Occupation

The spectacular magazine images of big game and the life-and-death nature struggles on television documentaries make the job of wildlife photographers seem glamorous and exciting. So do the travels of these professionals, who cross the globe, filming nature's fascinating creatures amid breathtaking scenery. Wyoming photographer Tom Mangelson travels nine months a year, often to exotic or remote locations. During a single twelve-week period in the spring, he flew to Alaska to photograph eagles and otters, to the Sea of Cortez off the coast of Mexico to shoot whales, dolphins, and sea lions, then to Hudson Bay in Canada to capture polar bears and arctic foxes on film, back down to Arizona to photograph songbirds, and finally to Wyoming to document the lives of wolves. His cameras whirred almost nonstop through those expeditions, taking 15,000 photographs.

Freelance photojournalist Michael Nichols once took four trips to India in seven months for a *National Geographic* magazine photo assignment on tigers. He spent over $300,000 on the project. Noel Rowe traveled to twenty countries in four years to produce a book of color photos of all 234 living species of primates. He was so enchanted by the project that he and his wife spent their honeymoon along Africa's Niger River while Noel tried to get photographs of the rare red colobus monkey.

Scientist, Hunter, Poet

There is another part to wildlife photography, however, the part the public does not see. For example, Patricia Caulfield, an Iowa native

who left a job as an editor at *Modern Photographer* magazine to pursue wildlife photography, took on the assignment of photographing the red wolf of the southern United States. Few people living today have ever seen one in the wild.

Caulfield knew better than to hope that she could stumble across this rare, wary animal that was active primarily after dark. She decided her best chance for a photo was to set up a camera trap in which the camera lens was connected to a trip wire. When the wolf bumped the wire, this would trigger a flash photograph.

Day after day, Caulfield drove out to the East Texas plain and slogged through the wet ground, slapping at clouds of mosquitoes as she searched for the type of habitat that a red wolf would prefer. Eventually, she settled on two locations, 50 miles (80 kilometers) apart.

The nearest was 75 miles (120 kilometers) from the town where Caulfield had set up her field headquarters. Since field mice often chewed on the wires, she had to go out each day to check the traps and repair the wires, if necessary. That meant 250 miles (400 kilometers) of driving simply to check two traps.

After a few weeks of checking the traps, Caulfield was thrilled to discover that one of the cameras had gone through half a roll of film. The trip wire had worked!

She sped down the highway 150 miles (240 kilometers) to the Houston airport. At considerable expense, she got the film on an airplane bound for her magazine, so the professionals there could develop the film. Eagerly, she waited for the report on how her photographs had turned out.

Wildlife photographers often travel to exotic and remote places to get a shot. Peggy and Erwin Bauer caught up with these king penguins on a subantarctic island.

Before the day was out, she got the answer. Her camera trap had captured the startled faces of toads, an otter, and a muskrat— but no red wolf.

A few days later, Caulfield discovered that a trap had shot an entire roll during the night. Having been burned by her previous experience, she went to a local photo service to develop the film. This time, she had captured the playful antics of a pack of Boy Scouts on a camp-out. After six weeks of work and still no sign of a red wolf, Caulfield had to give up the project.

Wildlife photographers do enjoy their work, but as the red wolf project shows, there is far more to their craft than hiking in the woods and pointing a camera at whatever appears. The work can be difficult, tedious, and financially unrewarding. Thomas Kennedy, director of photography for *National Geographic*, describes a good wildlife photographer as having the "mind of a scientist, the heart of a hunter, and the eyes of a poet. He is as persistent, adaptable, and hardy as the wild creatures he observers."

Rapid Rise of Wildlife Photography

Only in recent decades has wildlife photography become a profession at all. In the nineteenth century, cameras were clumsy and heavy. They were of use only when the subject was sitting completely still. As a result it was not practical to haul them out into the woods for the purpose of shooting wildlife. Not until around 1910 were portable cameras developed with fast enough shutters to allow taking pictures in the wild. Even then, the images were often so grainy, blurred, or shadowy that the result was disappointing.

Early wildlife photographers Frank and John Craighead climbed a precipitous cliff above the Potomac River to get this rare shot of a nesting falcon for *National Geographic* magazine in 1937.

Although better equipment and techniques gradually enabled photographers to create striking color photographs of animals, interest in these images was slow to develop. Until the late 1940s, photographs of wild animals were considered novelty items by all but a few dedicated nature lovers. Most serious photographers wanted nothing to do with wildlife photographers. This disdain caused even some of the best wildlife photographers to make a point of avoiding the label of wildlife photographer.

The 1970s, however, brought about a renewed interest in and awareness of the environment. Wildlife photographers contributed to this by providing illustrations of the amazing variety of creatures with whom we share our world. Their works helped the public to see the beauty and value of these animals and produced outrage over the fact that many of these animals were in danger of disappearing from Earth forever. Nature writer Bill McKibben has gone as far as to say, "Without Kodak [camera film], there would be no Endangered Species Act," a law passed by Congress that forbids the killing of animals whose existence as a species is in serious danger.

By increasing appreciation for nature and animals, wildlife photographers contributed to the explosive growth of their own field. More and more magazines wanted animal stories and photographs. Television networks demanded more specials and documentaries on animals. Currently, the demand is higher than ever for wildlife photographs and film.

Tough But Rewarding Field

Eight months after starting his career in 1971, Gunter Ziesler was nearly broke and driving a taxi to earn money to pay the bills. But in those days, eventually an enterprising outdoorsperson with a camera could expect to be professionally successful. After a tough start, Ziesler was able to make a good living from his photographs.

Today, the field is much more crowded. Despite the high demand for pictures, it is difficult to make a full-time career of photographing animals. Thousands of amateurs now take photographs for their own pleasure and some of them eventually find markets for their best pictures. Travel to remote locations has become easier and less expensive, allowing freelancers to flood the animal parks and refuges of the world. Tour guides in popular wildlife refuges such as the Serengeti preserve in Tanzania and Kenya provide facilities and assistance for would-be photographers.

With so many pictures flooding the market, all but a few of the most celebrated photographers have difficulty earning a steady income. Competition for acceptance by the few magazines and photo agencies that pay well is fierce. Even some of the best wildlife photographers are forced to give seminars, lead photo tours, and sell photographic equipment to help make ends meet.

The life of a wildlife photographer can be an adventure with rewards beyond measure. But those who succeed must be determined enough to overcome hardship and resourceful enough to meet extraordinary challenges.

"**Without Kodak [camera film],** there would be no Endangered Species Act," a law passed by Congress that forbids the killing of animals whose existence as a species is in serious danger.

Falling Under the Spell:
The Beginning Photographer

Asurprising number of top animal photographers in the world have found themselves in that line of work quite by accident. An interest in nature led many to photograph animals as a hobby. Eventually, they became so captivated by the freedom of the outdoor life, the adventure of stalking game with a camera, the beauty of the natural world, or the urgency of helping save the disappearing wild creatures of the Earth that they made it their life's work.

The call of the wild. Like many wildlife photographers, Jack Swedberg, formerly a carpenter, made a career change to join the ranks of the pros.

CHAPTER 2

Some photo-

graphers were

hunters who

found more

satisfaction in

**stalking
animals
with a
camera**

than with a rifle.

Career Change

Some of the best wildlife photographers were actively engaged in careers that had nothing to do with either the outdoors or photography before the bug hit. Jack Swedberg was a carpenter in Massachusetts before he chased after the dream of wildlife photography. Frans Lanting earned a master's degree in environmental economics in his native Netherlands in 1977. A year later he traveled to the United States to take courses at the University of California at Santa Cruz that would prepare him for a career in environmental planning. By 1980, he was so intrigued by the field of wildlife photography that he abandoned his studies and pursued it full time.

Wendell and Lucie Chapman spent eleven years in the business world. During their summer vacations, they liked to camp out in the wilderness and observe the animals. They came back with so many incredible stories about wildlife that some of their friends wondered if they were stretching their tales a bit. "Why don't you bring back a few pictures so we can believe you?" one suggested. The Chapmans accepted the challenge and took a camera along on their next trip. They became so captivated by wildlife photography that they switched careers.

After working hard for a doctoral degree in genetics and working for four years in this field in Mississippi, Dan Guravich realized that photography was his true passion. He began his new career by taking photographs for some of his agricultural clients. Working his way up to better jobs, he earned a position as official photographer for an expedition that was retracing historic efforts to find the fabled Northwest Passage through North America. On that journey, he saw his first polar bear. He was so entranced by these animals that he eventually shot photographs for four books on the bears of the Arctic.

Frederick Truslow is perhaps the ultimate example of someone who never expected to find himself in the field of wildlife photography. As a business manager, Truslow worked his way up the corporate ladder until he was managing nine manufacturing plants for a large New York corporation. The stress of the job, however, took such a toll on his health that his doctor urged him to change his lifestyle. Truslow turned to a hobby that he found both challenging and relaxing—wildlife photography. At the age of fifty-three, he turned this hobby into a career that brought him international praise.

Reformed Hunters

Some photographers were hunters who found more satisfaction in stalking animals with a camera than with a rifle. In the early 1900s, Jim Corbett earned a world reputation as a tiger hunter. But late in his career, he set aside his gun and shot only photographs of the striped jungle cats, becoming one of the first accomplished wildlife photographers in history.

More recently, when Jack Swedberg made his career switch from carpentry to photography, he also discontinued hunting as a hobby.

Jack Swedberg not only gave up carpentry for photography, he also gave up hunting. Now he finds getting shots such as the young doe hiding in the grass (above) more challenging and rewarding.

"With hunting, you either hit or miss," says Swedberg, "but photography is much more challenging." Swedberg found it so fascinating that he went into the business full time.

Childhood Interest

Other wildlife photographers deliberately pursued a career in wildlife photography, most often because of a childhood interest in nature. Tom Mangelson grew up with a father who was an enthusiastic outdoorsman. Although he claimed to be hunting, the elder Mangelson would sit in a blind along the Platte River near their Nebraska home, watching wildlife for an entire weekend without once lifting his gun. Tom developed the same appreciation for nature. This led him to study zoology and wildlife biology in college, and eventually he began photographing the subjects of his studies.

Gunter Ziesler's family had no use for nature during his childhood in Munich, Germany. But at the age of three or four, he came across pictures of African wildlife and fell in love with animals. At nineteen, Ziesler expanded on his attraction for animals by photographing them in zoos. Photography was strictly a hobby for him until he visited the Lake Mangas bird sanctuary in Turkey twelve years later. A professional photographer happened to be at Lake Mangas at the time. Ziesler became envious when he learned the man was spending three months at the bird sanctuary and that he made a living photographing wildlife. The young Ziesler decided then and there that he would try it, too.

Hugo van Lawick, an award-winning director and producer of animal films, knew nothing about cameras or wildlife photography when he took his first animal photos. Born in Indonesia of Dutch descent, he was walking with friends in a national park in The Netherlands when they saw a wild sheep. One friend had a camera and wanted a close-up picture. Since van Lawick was good at approaching wildlife without scaring them, he crawled on his stomach through a blueberry field to get the shot. He so enjoyed the adventure that he and three friends joined together to form a wildlife film team.

Related Fields

Some photographers moved into wildlife photography as a natural offshoot of their professional training. Jim Brandenburg earned a degree in studio art from the University of Minnesota at Duluth. Upon leaving school, he found a job in his field, as a picture editor for a newspaper in the small town of Worthington, Minnesota.

Over the years, Brandenburg's work in photography attracted interest from major magazines. *National Geographic*, for example, assigned him to shoot photographs for a feature on China in 1978. Eight years later, the same magazine hired him to photograph white wolves in the wild. Brandenburg grew so attached to the white wolves that he spent years focusing his camera on wildlife.

Noel Rowe came into the career from the opposite end. The Connecticut-born Rowe studied marine science at Southampton College in Long Island, New York, in the 1970s. For several years, he pursued his chosen career at the New York Ocean Science Laboratory. His interest in studying animals triggered an interest in photographing them, and he went to school to learn about photography. By the time he finished the classes, he was driven by the dream of photographing all the world's primates.

Amos Nachoum was not thinking of either wildlife or photography when he enlisted in the Israeli armed forces. But during his training as a special diver for the navy, he was taught to operate an underwater camera. This sparked an interest in photographing undersea life that led him to become one of the world's experts in this field.

Becoming Wise in the Ways of Animals

Stories such as those of Truslow and the Chapmans make it appear that almost anyone can become a wildlife photographer with little or no training. It is true that some have succeeded with little formal training in the animal sciences. That does not, however, mean that knowledge and skill in those areas is unnecessary. It simply means that unusually motivated people have been able to gain that expertise on their own. Some, such as van Lawick, read every book about animals that they could find. Others such as Truslow and the Chapmans developed their understanding of wildlife over many years of careful personal observation.

All of the experts stress that a person interested in mastering wildlife photography must understand how animals live and why they behave the way they do. North Carolina native John Shaw, who has gained a reputation as "master of the close-up," explains, "The more you know about nature, the more you will see to photograph."

Some advise studying this in a formal manner, by going for a doctorate or master's degree in biology. Others suggest trying to combine photography with some other kind of scientific work. For example, a person could develop both nature expertise and photography skills by documenting field research with birds or wild animals.

But even those who urge formal study of animals and photography agree that there is no substitute for personal knowledge of animals and their habitat gained from experience in the field. Like trained naturalists, most wildlife experts keep careful records of what they see, including locations of animals, animal behavior, and weather and habitat conditions, on every trip out into nature. A

Jim Brandenburg came upon this arctic wolf with pup while trekking across Ellesmere Island in Canada's Northwest Territories. Such encounters led Brandenburg to change his career from a professional photographer to a wildlife photographer.

How the Lens Works

The word "photography" means "to write with light," and the main camera skill that a photographer must learn is how to control the amount of light to which the film is exposed. The two features that control this are the aperture, or size of the lens opening, and the shutter speed.

The aperture is measured in a number known as the f-stop. The larger the f-stop number, the smaller the lens opening. A small f-stop lets in a great deal of light while a large f-stop lets in little. The shutter speed determines how long the film is exposed to light. A slow shutter speed lets in much light, a fast shutter speed allows little. Photographers use a light meter to measure the amount of light available for a shot. Veteran photographers can then make their own lighting adjustments based on their experience with a particular background or subject.

There are two other effects of aperture and shutter control. A small lens opening brings more of the scene into focus, while a large opening brings only objects at a certain distance into focus. A slow shutter speed tends to blur moving objects, while a fast shutter speed can bring even a fast-flying bird into sharp focus.

person who does not enjoy spending long periods of time in the wild cannot develop a feel for capturing the world of nature on film. He or she will not know where to look, when to look, what certain behaviors mean, or what is worth photographing.

Learning to Use the Camera

While some professionals have been trained in the use of cameras, many have gained their expertise through experience. The best of the best have lots of expensive equipment such as special lenses for superclose-ups and underwater shots, and such features as remote control that allows the operation of a camera from a distance. However, experts say that there are only three pieces of equipment needed for taking high-quality nature shots:

The first is the camera. Any basic 35-millimeter camera from a major manufacturer will do.

The second essential need for a wildlife photographer is a collection of lenses. A telephoto lens is especially important for getting close, highly detailed photographs of animals that are wary of humans.

The third important piece of equipment is a tripod. While most amateur photographers are used to holding a camera while shooting, not even the steadiest hand can keep a camera absolutely still. John Shaw maintains, "Every working professional nature photographer shoots every exposure possible with his or her camera mounted on a tripod." Handheld shots are used only in situations where a tripod is not feasible, such as when shooting from a vehicle, underwater photographs, and sudden opportunities where there is no time for setting up the shot.

Equipped with essential gear (camera, good lens, and tripod), Peggy Bauer pursues wildlife in Denali National Park, Alaska.

Gaining Experience

Wildlife photographers do not generally book a flight to the African grasslands to start their collection of animal pictures. Even the top professionals have found that one of the best locations for learning field photography is a nearby woods, marsh, or meadow. "You may never film trumpeter swans on a frigid morning in Yellowstone National Park," says Joe McDonald, "but you may have many chances to photograph mallards or Canada geese on a cold morning at a nearby city park."

In fact, say the experts, the closer to the photographer's home, the better. Easy access to a location allows them to visit it frequently, and to become familiar with the terrain and with the wildlife in that area. Good photographs of birds can even be obtained by shooting in their backyards.

Pros who want to gain experience shooting animals not found in their area often frequent the national parks. These wilderness areas have good roads and camping accommodations. In addition, thousands of tourists visit these parks every year. Therefore the animals are more used to the presence of humans and are generally less shy than those in remote wilderness areas.

The wildlife photographer need not travel far to get great wildlife shots. Sometimes birds like this meadowlark turn up right in the backyard.

CHAPTER 3

Getting Close

Nature documentaries that show wild animals hunting, chasing, and killing their prey give a misleading impression of wildlife photography. The average outdoor enthusiast may spend a lifetime in the field without ever coming across such a scene. Many wild animals depend on stealth for their survival and are so good at staying hidden that they are seldom glimpsed, even by someone with powerful binoculars. "To be present in the field for a significant happening in an animal's life is usually more difficult than finding a needle in a haystack," says Pat Caulfield.

To find and get close enough to capture these elusive creatures on film, wildlife photographers must be skilled detectives and hunters. Like any skilled detective, some of their most important work is done before they ever

By wedging himself into a hole in the mountainside, Frederick Truslow was able to capture these elusive California condors as they alighted on a branch.

set up a camera. Photographers spend considerable time researching and observing their subjects and the habitats in which they live. Only when they discover the behavior patterns of the animals can photographers figure out how to break down what some call the invisible wall that exists between humans and many wild creatures that regard humans as intruders in their world.

Favorite Haunts

One of the most important skills is the ability to recognize when animals have been to a certain spot, and whether or not they are likely to return. Frederick Truslow's expertise in this area allowed him to photograph a rare California condor. The condors are extremely wary of humans and have superb eyesight. That meant that Truslow could not hope to get a good photograph by walking around and looking for condors. Instead, he explored a region where condors were known to roost until he found a pine bough splattered with fresh condor droppings. Figuring that the bird would eventually return to familiar haunts, Truslow squeezed into a hole in the mountainside near the tree and waited with his camera. Eventually, a condor did alight on the branch, and Truslow got his photographs.

On another occasion, Truslow relied on an expert's familiarity with the behavior of his subject—a large waterbird called an anhinga. Anhingas need a place to stand and dry their feathers after feeding in the water. Truslow's friend noticed a turtle crawling up on a rock that he recognized as an anhinga's drying spot. He advised Truslow to focus his camera on the rock. As the expert anticipated, an anhinga arrived within minutes, furious at finding an intruder on its favorite spot. The tip allowed Truslow to capture wonderful shots of the bird attacking and driving off the turtle.

The Blind

The most common way photographers get close to animals in the wild is to use a blind. A blind is a small enclosed structure that shields a person from the view of animals. Blinds work particularly well with birds whose excellent eyesight usually detects movement when a photographer tries to set up or advance closer.

Some of the earliest nature photographers spent countless hours building blinds made to look exactly like trees, rocks, or other animals. Some modern-day photographers copy those methods. Jack Swedberg likes to go out in the water of marshlands without being seen. For this he builds a blind that looks like a hummock—a free-floating mat of grass and vegetation common in marshlands, which he can push in the water. Swedberg constructs the hummock blind out of chicken wire and plywood, then covers it with cattails and grasses found on real hummocks. He then puts on hip boots and wades into the water. Shielded by the hummock blind, he can get close-up shots of wildlife from a unique view of only a foot or so above the water.

Photographer Swedberg utilized his carpentry skills to painstakingly fashion a natural-looking hummock out of branches.

But photographers have found that, for most species, blinds do not have to blend in exactly with the surroundings. The most common type of portable blind is one constructed of aluminum or bamboo legs with a covering stretched over it. The covering must not have any loose material that might flap in the wind and scare off wildlife. This type of blind is light enough to carry long distances through rugged terrain. It can be set up almost anywhere—in snow, even on stilts in wetlands—in less than three minutes. Many photographers who work in national parks and game refuges, where the road winds close to nature, use their automobiles as blinds.

Blinds are of no use if animals suspect a person is in them. Photographers must enter the blind without being seen. The only

Here Jack Swedberg positions himself in a floating blind to await the arrival of his subjects.

way to ensure arriving before most animals are out and about is to get into the blind well before the first light of day. Furthermore, photographers often do not leave until after the animals have left, especially if they want to return to the site. This may require staying in the blind until it gets dark.

Space is limited in a blind. There is usually only enough room for one person to sit or lie down as he or she peers through a small rectangular window slot. Since they may have to spend all day in the blind, photographers try to make themselves as comfortable as possible. They often bring along a stool, and food and drink. In cold weather they may bring along a portable propane heater and a small stove for coffee. Some put pieces of carpet on the ground, but that serves more to muffle sounds than to provide comfort.

Limitations of Blinds

There are times when even a blind will not get photographers close enough to an animal to capture the photos they want, such as a close-up view of eggs hatching in a nest. In such cases, and with a great deal of advance preparation, photographers can hide a remote camera near the viewing area that they can operate from a distance so that the subject never detects their presence.

Some wildlife refuges have permanent blinds, left over from research projects, set up at water holes and other places animals frequent. These work for photographing mammals as well as birds because the animals have become used to humans over many years of study. But as a rule, blinds are not as successful with mammals as they are with birds because mammals rely more on their sense of smell than on sight. Gerry Lemmo discovered this on a freezing winter day. After a long trek by snowmobile into the Adirondack Mountains, Lemmo cleared away the deep snow to set up his tent blind facing a stream bank where weasels had been reported. After waiting for hours for the creatures to show up, he was startled to see a curious weasel pop its head into the blind!

Stalking

Mammals' relatively poor vision often makes it possible to approach them on foot. The first rule of stalking a mammal is to steer clear of its sense of smell. Wildlife photographers always approach from downwind so their scent will carry away from the animal. They avoid using tobacco, as well as strong aftershaves or deodorants. Many of them will dab themselves with animal scents.

The second rule is to avoid sudden movement. Even mammals that do not see well can detect motion. Photographers never walk directly toward an animal in the wild unless it is looking the other way or is occupied with eating.

Some wildlife photographers have found that mammals are too sensitive to smell and movement for them to sneak up on them. They prefer to come right out in the open with what one photographer calls the "ambling-along-without-a-care" approach. They never approach the animal directly and act as though they are not interested in the creature at all. Gradually, over the course of days or even weeks, the animal becomes used to the human's presence and the photographer is able to get close enough to take good photos without spooking the subject.

Knowing how to recognize signs of animal behavior is important in stalking. "How an animal reacts to you one day might be completely different the next," notes Frans Lanting. If the animals appear nervous, experienced photographers will make no further effort to approach and simply sit and wait until the creatures appear to be more at ease.

Lures and Decoys

Many photographers set up their equipment in a spot that an animal is likely to approach and then use lures or decoys to attract their subjects. A lure is usually food or a scent that an animal will find irresistible. An animal's favorite food works best if it is laid out just before the creature's preferred feeding times—usually around sunrise and sunset. Photographers, however, must use care to avoid contaminating the bait with their own scent.

Jack Swedberg had good success photographing eagles with a combination of blind and lures. He covered his plywood blind with beaver cuttings from a nearby pond so that it blended with its surroundings. Then he placed a newly found deer carcass on the ice in front of the blind to attract the eagles. Finally, knowing that an eagle's eyesight is sharp enough to detect the silent motion of a closing camera shutter, he scattered dried corn near the blind. This attracted small birds, whose movement distracted the eagles' attention away from any small motions the photographer might make.

A decoy is an artificial device meant to fool an animal into thinking it is real. Duck hunters have used decoys in the shape of ducks to attract their quarry for many years. Photographers more commonly use noise decoys, particularly with birds. They may play tapes of birds to attract those of the same species, or tapes of an owl, which attracts songbirds intent on mobbing or driving out the intruder. Taped decoys, however, are illegal at most parks and wildlife refuges.

Traps and Remotes

Especially elusive animals may require the kind of camera traps described in Chapter 1. The elusive animal includes not only those that are wary but also those that are active only at night and those whose movements are too fast for a person to follow—such as insects in flight. In a camera trap, the shutter is activated when an animal comes in contact with a triggering mechanism. The triggers range from a simple wire that the animal brushes against to invisible photoelectric beams designed by electronics engineers at a cost of tens of thousands of dollars. Camera traps often include lures to bring the animals into contact with the cameras, and scents to mask the smell of the humans who set them up. Their main drawback is the fact that they are "hit-or-miss" devices—the camera often can take only one photograph before the animal is frightened off, especially if it's a night camera that requires a flash.

Alternate Methods

A wildlife photographer with good contacts in the field can save countless hours of futile searching for animals. On one project, Pat Caulfield was able to get photographs of the camera-shy sandhill crane after receiving a tip from a Florida rancher that a pair returned to a section of his pasture every year. Forest rangers, naturalists, hunters, and wildlife researchers are also good sources of information about animal locations.

Some of the best photographs of rare and endangered species have been taken on the few occasions when members of the species are released into the wild. This may occur when an injured animal has been healed or when a young animal raised in captivity is set free. Knowing about a planned release of a Florida panther allowed Caulfield to set up her camera in advance at the site of the release to get rare shots of the vanishing species.

Wildlife photographers do not always go into the wilderness to get pictures. Some take photographs of animals in zoos, which often provide a natural setting for the animals. Others build a large

enclosed set that looks like a wilderness and photograph the subjects that they place inside of it. Shots of predators capturing prey, which would be difficult to get in nature, are frequently obtained in such artificial settings. Such methods, however, have produced a heated debate about whether they produce valid wildlife shots or whether they distort nature and provide false images of the natural world (see Chapter 7).

To get this rare shot of an endangered Florida panther, Pat Caulfield waited for its planned release by wildlife researchers.

CHAPTER 4

Hardships

For every vivid animal photograph published in a magazine, there are hundreds, perhaps thousands, of lesser quality that had to be thrown away. For every fascinating second of wildlife behavior shown on television, there are minutes, perhaps hours, of film thrown in the trash. And for every roll of film shot, a photographer may have spent many minutes, perhaps hours, sitting and waiting for the right moment.

Hours of waiting in the swamp paid off when Jack Swedberg captured this brief skirmish between two American alligators on film.

While the job of a wildlife photographer may sound glamorous, the experts spent most of their time in the field watching and waiting, often in miserable conditions. Lions, for example, sleep about twenty hours a day. A person trying to get a photo of a lion actually doing something significant is generally in for a long wait.

Yet the action, when it comes, may be over in the flash of a paw. Throughout those long hours of waiting, a photographer must have a camera loaded and ready to shoot at all times. An instant of daydreaming can spoil a moment for which a photographer has waited weeks. Jack Swedberg once waited through hours of numbing inactivity while observing alligators in a Florida swamp. Suddenly, one of the alligators attacked another. The action lasted only a few brief seconds, and had Swedberg not been alert and ready, he would have missed it.

The Long, Lonely Wait

The ability of top wildlife photographers to bide their time waiting for the right moment is legendary. Michael Nichols once spent three weeks sitting in a tree in the Congo to get a single photograph of a lowland gorilla in the water. As Gunter Ziesler says, "Patience is probably the most important attribute of a wildlife photographer."

Nature photographers seldom have any human company to break up the long days of waiting in the field. As difficult as it is for one person to keep quiet and avoid frightening off skittish wildlife, the task would be greatly magnified for a group of people. While some wildlife photographers would agree with Ziesler when he says, "I am happiest when I am working on my own, when I see nobody at all," most must learn to cope with the silence and loneliness required to

Against an East African backdrop, Frans Lanting captured these giraffes with necks crossed.

get close to wild animals. Often, they pass the time pleasantly by noting all kinds of activity that the average hiker would miss, such as subtle changes of color in a field from a passing cloud.

Most photographers find it hard enough just getting good photographs of wild creatures. Tom Mangelson makes his task even more difficult by trying for that special shot that truly captures the majesty of the animal in its natural setting. One of his favorite methods is to select the perfect natural setting for a photograph and then wait for wildlife to come into view. He may sit for ten hours at a time at a location, always on the alert for the fleeting moment when his subject appears.

On one occasion, Mangelson was determined to capture an Alaskan brown bear in the act of swallowing a salmon. He waited in the same spot by a stream from dawn until dusk for an entire week before he got the shot. Another time, he spent two weeks looking out from a mountain peak near the Chilkat River in Alaska, waiting for an eagle to fly into his chosen backdrop.

For photographers such as Frans Lanting, the waiting game begins before he even thinks about picking up his camera. Lanting prefers to spend a long time at a single location to become familiar with the terrain, the landscape, and the animals. Even more important, he waits until the animals have become familiar with him before he approaches them with a camera. He may spend weeks standing in one area before the wildlife finally accept his presence.

Noel Rowe used a similar approach when he set out to photograph all the primates of the world. For him, the most difficult part of his entire project was trying to ease the animals away from their natural fear of humans. Rowe followed some species around all day for months until they finally became convinced he was no threat to them.

Foul Weather

The long waits would be difficult enough for most people even if they were seated on a plush sofa in a cozy room. The wilderness, however, does not cater to human creature comforts. Wildlife photographers have to stand up to some of the worst weather, terrain, and pests that nature can offer.

Constant rain is one of the most difficult elements. In addition to the discomfort of sitting through days of endless showers, photographers have to take special care to keep their equipment dry. Frederick Truslow once traveled to Aransas National Wildlife Refuge in Texas to photograph that last remaining colony of wild whooping cranes. Whenever he got set up for a shot, gray skies would move in and the rains poured down for days on end. Truslow stuck it out for seven months, hoping for a day when both the birds and weather would cooperate. Finally, on an April day, the sun came out. Truslow rushed to his blind and finished all the photography for the project in three hours.

Photographers may have to sit outdoors in sweltering heat, hike in ice and hailstorms, and plod through hip-deep mud. Most of

Joel Sartore endured a plague of sweat bees and other hardships to photograph jungle wildlife in Bolivia's Madidi National Park.

them have experienced the ordeal of fending off clouds of mosquitoes or biting flies while trying to hold steady for a photo. But, generally, they accept the hardships as a small price to pay for the love of nature. Some find the waiting to be calming, relaxing, even fascinating. Nebraska native Joel Sartore, who specializes in photographing endangered animals, shrugged off the six cold weeks in winter he spent trying to get close to wolves in Yellowstone National Park. The hardship was hardly noticeable because, he says, "I got to enjoy the park every day."

Tom Mangelson handles the hardships of outdoor living by adopting a defiant attitude. He has shot film in the Arctic when the temperature plunged to $-30°F$ ($-35°C$), and his hands were frostbitten as he tried to reload his camera in a snowstorm. He has taken photos in torrents of rain blown nearly sideways by driving winds and has roamed the wilderness in hailstorms. Yet Mangelson claims it's all in a day's work.

"I work in terrible weather so often I don't think of it as terrible weather," he says. "I think of it as normal." In fact, Mangelson occasionally goes out of his way to lug his camera out into the worst possible conditions. He prefers depicting animals coping with the harsh realities of nature such as rainstorms and blizzards.

Health Hazards

Harsh wilderness conditions become even more difficult to bear when illness strikes. Unfortunately, disease is an occupational hazard for those photographers who work in remote, damp regions.

Malaria, a disease carried by mosquitoes, is a constant danger in many of the world's swamps and marshes. Michael Nichols has come down with the disease more than a dozen times in his career. Frans Lanting caught a case of malaria while working in

Madagascar, but the symptoms did not show up until he left the island and arrived in Antarctica to photograph penguins. By then it was too late to turn back. Camping by himself, and with no medication available, Lanting grew sicker and sicker. "By the time the boat came back for me days later," he remembers, "I was too weak to stand and walk."

Nichols faced a different but equally miserable experience in Africa. He sat all day next to a swamp, trying to get photographs of gorillas and never noticed that small parasites called footworms were burrowing into his skin. "They don't itch until they start moving," Nichols explains. "Then you know they're traveling." The worms burrowed through his skin and created large itching welts all over his body.

Frustration

It is not only the harsh realities of nature that pose problems for those who earn their living with a camera. Frustration can also seep in from the civilized world. Art Wolfe is a successful photographer who once spent a month photographing wildlife in the desert Southwest of the United States. While driving back to his home in Seattle, he stopped for lunch in San Francisco. He returned to his car to find someone had broken into it. His entire month's work captured in six hundred rolls of film was gone.

Another source of frustration is transportation headaches. The search for rare animals often leads wildlife photographers to places where transportation is either poor or does not exist at all. Frequently, they have to charter their own planes and hire drivers or boat pilots or guides. In attempting to get to his destination at Botswana's Okavanga Delta, Frans Lanting had to improvise his transportation. He made arrangements to have an old, overgrown, and long out-of-use mission site cleared so that his chartered plane could land.

Frans Lanting caught a case of malaria while working in Madagascar, but the symptoms did not show up until he left the island and arrived in Antarctica to photograph penguins. **By then it was too late to turn back.**

Most wildlife photographers are not able to spend as much time in the wild as they would like. Routine and mundane tasks such as sorting slides, submitting photographs to publishers, keeping records, and developing proposals are necessary, time-consuming tasks for a photographer who hopes to stay in business.

Of all the hardships and frustrations that a wildlife photographer can face, nothing causes more anguish than coming back empty-handed. When Noel Rowe caught sight of a Sumatran orangutan, a rare and endangered species, he excitedly moved in to capture it on film. But when he set up his tripod, it slowly began to sink in the soft ground. No matter where he set it up, the stand would shift or sink immediately. At long last, he found a place where the tripod would stay, only to have his subject turn its head away. Rowe waited and waited, but the orangutan refused to face the camera. "I think he just didn't want to be photographed," said Rowe. "It was incredibly frustrating."

The Photo Makes It All Worthwhile

On the other hand wildlife photographers will gladly put up with almost any difficulty so long as they get the shot they are after. Tom Mangelson wanted to photograph a sandhill crane's egg in the process of hatching. He chartered two airplane flights with small-plane pilots and then hitched a boat ride with an Inuit family in his search in western Alaska for a sandhill crane nest. He then hiked for 10 miles (16 kilometers) a day through the soggy tundra marsh, with never a solid flat place to step.

Fifteen days later, he found what he was looking for. Not wanting to scare off the notoriously wary birds, he built a series of blinds. Over the course of three weeks, much of it in pouring rain, Mangelson gradually moved his camera forward to the nearest blind.

He waited there for four days, now so low on food that he was 20 pounds (9 kilograms) lighter than when he arrived for the shoot.

Finally, his patience appeared to pay off as an egg began to hatch. Mangelson peered through his lens only to find that the constant rain had caused so much condensation on his lens that he could not see a thing. By the time he got the lens cleared, the bird had hatched and was out of the nest. Mangelson had not managed to get a single shot!

It was not until ten years later that he found another sandhill crane nest, on a river in Idaho. Mangelson got the photographs, and when he saw the finished product, he declared that the long search, with all its frustrations, had been well worth the effort. But he probably agreed with early wildlife photographer George Shiras, the first person to use a trip cord for wildlife photography, who once said, "No one completes an assignment; you survive it."

PREVIOUS PAGES Tom Mangelson's fascination with sandhill cranes took him on long treks throughout Canada and the United States. Along the Platte River he came upon these cranes feeding. ABOVE A young sandhill chick hides in the vegetation.

Danger!

In the early decades of the twentieth century, photographers took huge risks when they set about to get pictures of large wild animals. Since there were no telephoto lenses, they had to set up their cameras dangerously close to their subjects. Carl Ackeley, who shot big-game photographs for the American Museum of Natural History, was perhaps the first to die on the job, from injuries suffered when an elephant attacked him.

Wildlife photographer Nicole Duplaix faced these charging elephants while photographing in Kruger National Park, South Africa.

CHAPTER 5

Even with telephoto lenses that allow photographers to get close-ups from great distances, modern wildlife photographers continue to run risks that the animals they stalk will turn on them. The desire to get closer and see more is almost irresistible.

An expert wildlife photographer usually has a good feel for when a wild animal feels threatened by an intruder. "Every animal gives off signals, often through its body language, that tells you when to back off," says Frans Lanting. But even the most experienced outdoor expert can misread those signals. Peter Beard, a veteran photographer of the African nature scene, barely escaped death in September 1996 while photographing elephants in Kenya. One of the beasts trampled him, breaking his pelvis and goring him with a tusk.

An Angry Wolfpack

Joel Sartore has survived his share of close calls in the wild. He narrowly avoided being gored by a musk ox, and was once nearly squashed by a 2-ton walrus. But his most frightening adventure occurred when he got too close to a pack of wolves.

Sartore had been following the pack for several weeks in a remote section of Yellowstone National Park. Unable to get a good wolf picture for a number of days, he began to get impatient and approached a little closer than he normally would. One of the wolves got up and growled threateningly at him. Immediately, Sartore realized he had made a dangerous mistake. His truck was so far away that he had no chance of reaching it. Nor was there any tree or other haven of safety nearby.

The wolves began to surround him, all growling in an attack stance. Instinct told him to run for his life. But Sartore thought about his observations of wolves in their attacks on elks. The ones that had run for safety had almost always been killed. Those that stood their ground sometimes discouraged the wolves, who then went off in search of easier prey. Sartore triggered the flash on his camera and threw his hands in the air. The tactic worked. The wolves backed off and Sartore was able to get to safety, but was both shaken and embarrassed by the incident.

"No one in recorded history has ever been attacked by wolves in the lower 48 states," he said. "I would have been the first and it was completely my fault."

Chased by Antlers

Large antlered animals like moose and elk normally pose no great risk to people, so long as the animals are not provoked. But when such animals are in their mating or rutting season, their tempers become much more hair-triggered. Greg Pierson, a photographer from Texas, had to choose between his expensive camera and his survival when charged by an enraged bull elk during rutting season. Reluctantly, he ditched his camera.

Frederick Truslow's blunder almost got him battered by a bull moose during mating season at Isle Royale, an island in Lake Superior. With the help of a park ranger, he located a favorite spot of a pair of moose and moved in close enough to begin photographing. All went well until he made a clumsy move while shifting his tripod. The clinking sound startled the bull moose, who was furious at being disturbed during mating season.

The 1,600-pound (726-kilogram) animal tore after Truslow, who reached a small stand of trees in the nick of time. The moose's antlers got caught in the closely packed trees. While the animal shook himself free, Truslow was able to duck into a lean-to he had set up near his camp.

Unable to see the intruder, whose close presence he could smell, the moose was nearly beside himself with rage. The angry bull snorted and pawed the ground and spent fifteen minutes searching for Truslow. The hidden photographer snapped pictures until the animal finally left. "I was so scared I felt there was a lead ball in my stomach," said Truslow, "but I didn't get the shakes until it was all over."

Bear Attacks

Like most animals, bears avoid people most of the time. But occasionally one will lose its caution around humans and will even attack when unprovoked. Not even the most experienced woodsmen can predict when that will happen.

In August 1996, wildlife photographer Michio Hoshino camped out in the Kamchatka Peninsula in eastern Russia. A well-known expert in photographing bears and other wildlife of the northern forests, Hoshino was part of a Japanese team filming a television documentary. At four o'clock one morning, a large bear attacked his tent on the bank of a lake. It dragged Hoshino into the woods. By the time the rest of the crew was able to drive off the bear, Hoshino was dead.

Wendell Chapman was more fortunate in several close encounters with grizzly bears. On one occasion, he was engrossed in taking photos of a pack of bighorn sheep when he heard a clatter of rocks behind him. He turned and saw a horrifying sight. In his own words, "Two grizzlies, not fifty feet off, hair bristling, mouths open, galloped down upon me." A quick glance around revealed that there was no tree or cliff or anything else that might provide protection.

Groping for any means of survival, Chapman shouted and aimed his camera at the bears. As with Sartore and the wolves, this aggressive response apparently confused the bears, who halted 30 feet (9 meters) away. One of them rose up on its back legs to its full

Photographer Galen Rowel managed to get this great shot of an angry brown bear without mishap in Chilkat, Alaska.

height before it lumbered off. Chapman recognized a priceless shot of the bear silhouetted against a rugged mountain backdrop. Hoping that his camera was in focus, he snapped two pictures.

On another occasion, several grizzlies boldly overran the Chapmans' campground. Wendell and Lucie were in their trailer at the time. Realizing that a trailer filled with food was a grizzly bear magnet, the two tried desperately to frighten away the bears. But no matter how they flashed their searchlight and banged pots and pans, the bears continued prowling the camp. The Chapmans finally made a dash for their car and drove away.

Angry Rhino

Early in his career, Hugo van Lawick helped film an episode on catching a rhinoceros for a television series. The animal trappers drove full speed across the plain in a truck while one man on the truck held a noose attached to the end of a bamboo pole to catch the rhino. Van Lawick sat on the back of the truck trying to film the capture while holding on for dear life and ducking thornbushes that flashed by his face.

When the trappers slipped the noose over the rhino's head, that introduced a new danger. The angry rhinoceros charged the truck and lifted one side into the air, nearly toppling it. Van Lawick fought for his balance while keeping his camera running.

Other Harrowing Encounters

It is not just mammals that pose threats to photographers. Frans Lanting spent several days wading in chin-deep water in an African wetland, shooting eye-level photos of the habitat. When he returned to the spot a short time later, he was shocked to find a large crocodile living in the area he had waded through.

Frederick Truslow once sat in a blind waiting to film some whooping cranes when a water moccasin almost 5 feet (1.5 meters) long slithered into his cramped space. Truslow had to stand on his stool while he carefully nudged the big snake out with his tripod.

A Different Kind of Close Call

Truslow owes his life to his foresight in taking a walkie-talkie radio with him on a visit to a blind on another occasion, although the danger came from the elements rather than from any ferocious beasts. He spent several frustrating weeks at the Red Rock Lakes National Wildlife Refuge in Montana trying to photograph trumpeter swans, the world's largest waterfowl. The swans were so leery of humans that even though Truslow set up his blind a good 150 feet (45 meters) away from their nesting site, they would not approach the nesting area.

Unable to make any progress to ease the birds' suspicions, Truslow was packing up to leave the refuge when he noticed the nearby muskrat houses, covered with a plant called sedge. He arranged sedge on his blind and then gradually moved it in closer. The swans appeared to tolerate the blind even at a distance of 80 feet (24 meters).

Truslow then entered the blind, which was standing in nearly waist-high, icy water and waited for the ideal moment. After thirteen hours in the blind, Truslow prepared to leave only to find that long exposure to the water had temporarily paralyzed him from the waist down. Fortunately, with his walkie-talkie he was able to call a friend to find him and pull him out.

Such dedication to their craft is typical of top wildlife photographers. "The risk isn't important to me," says Michael Nichols. "It's the mission, the conservation message that's important."

Truslow then entered the blind, which was standing in nearly waist-high, icy water and **waited for the ideal moment.** After thirteen hours in the blind, Truslow prepared to leave only to find that long exposure to the water had temporarily paralyzed him from the waist down.

CHAPTER 6

Luck, Skill or Preparation?

Every wildlife photographer will admit that there is an element of luck to many of their best wildlife shots. In many cases, they just happened to be in the right spot at the right time when a rare animal appeared, or when animals did something unusual.

Frederick Truslow happened across some totally unexpected behavior while watching the nest of a pair of large pileated woodpeckers in Florida's Everglades. The birds had hollowed out a nest about two thirds of the way up a 30-foot (9-meter) dead tree. The hollowing apparently weakened the rotting tree so much that the top broke off, leaving the nest and the eggs exposed. As an amazed Truslow shot film from his perch in a 12-foot (3.6-meter) tower blind, a woodpecker picked up one of the eggs in its beak and flew off with it to a new location. The bird returned twice more to retrieve the other two eggs. No one had ever heard of a woodpecker doing such a thing, yet Truslow captured it all on film.

Photographers Jim Brandenburg and Stephen Durst were filming wolves in Canada when this jaeger put in an unexpected appearance, giving Durst an opportunity for a memorable shot.

Patience and Persistence

But being a wildlife photographer is not simply a matter of heading out into the outdoors and hoping to win nature's lottery. "Luck is an important ingredient," says photography expert Nigel Sitwell, "but good luck tends to come to those who already have what it takes in other ways."

Pat Caulfield stumbled upon the secret to a difficult shoot involving the notoriously secretive sandhill cranes, but only because she refused to quit in the face of defeat. The project started when a Florida cattle rancher tipped her off to a pair of cranes that returned every autumn to a boggy stretch of land in one of his pastures. For years, the rancher had been going out to that pasture at 8 A.M. to scatter corn for the birds. The cranes had come to trust the farmer enough to feed on the corn.

Knowing how difficult the cranes are to approach when nesting, Caulfield covered a blind with palmetto leaves that grew near the pasture. She then started out across the pasture at 7:15 A.M. so that she would be in place before the cranes arrived. But well before she reached the blind, she heard the birds' nervous calls. When the rancher arrived at eight and scattered corn, the cranes not only refused to eat it, they would not even come near the pasture.

Caulfield arose earlier and earlier each day to try to reach the blind before the suspicious birds arrived from their nests. Yet the birds always seemed alert to her coming. Once she started out across the pasture at 3:00 A.M. As she drew near the blind, a pleasant silence greeted her. At last, she had outsmarted the cranes, she thought. But just before she got to the blind she heard the cranes call out their warning.

Caulfield tried other tacks. She dressed in the rancher's clothes to fool the cranes. Still the cranes refused to come near the blind. The photographer was nearly ready to give up, but she tried a last approach. She walked with the rancher as the man scattered the corn to the blind. The rancher went into the blind with Caulfield and then left. Caulfield stayed behind. Although she was certain the cranes were not fooled into thinking the blind was empty, nonetheless the birds came to feed on the corn, and Caulfield had her photographs.

Skill

Amos Nachoum combined his outstanding skill as a diver with a stroke of luck to capture some fascinating pictures of humpback whales. Snorkeling off the coast of an island in the South Pacific, Nachoum had the good fortune to come across a mother whale caring for its two-week-old calf. Nachoum dove 40 feet (12 meters) beneath the surface to find a good angle for his photograph. Were he not able to hold his breath under the sea for over a minute, he would not have succeeded in capturing the playful affection of a mother whale for its calf.

Frans Lanting noticed a group of shorebirds gathering in the same area at the edge of the water every time the tide was high. The flat, open beach offered no cover at all for a photographer. He avoided scaring them by stretching out flat and crawling through 50 yards (45 meters) of surf, an inch at a time. When he got close enough, he used his elbows for a tripod.

His best photograph of the day was one of a marbled godwit that descended straight into the camera and landed only feet away. It was more than luck, however, that put Lanting in position to get the shot. From his long experience with shorebirds, Lanting knew that they liked to make their landings into the wind. He had crawled with the wind behind his back in hopes that he could get a full frontal view of a bird landing.

Truslow was also able to get a photograph of a black skimmer flying with its beak in the water. Again, it was more than luck that made it happen. The photographer knew that this particular bird slits the water with its beak on a flyby to attract fish, then comes

around a second time to scoop up those fish. Truslow simply focused on a leaf floating in the water near a spot where a skimmer had just passed and was ready and waiting when the bird returned.

Preparation

Most outstanding photos take a great deal of advanced preparation. Jim Brandenburg's images of five-week-old arctic wolf pups venturing out for the first time to play in the snow occurred only after weeks of careful study into the habits and behavior of the wolves.

For those photographers who do not have the luxury of a guaranteed assignment from a magazine or some other sponsor, the preparation may begin more than a year ahead of the actual photos. When Pat Caulfield got the idea of shooting photos of prairie dogs, she began by researching her subject at the American Museum of Natural History in New York City. From the information she gathered, she decided to concentrate on two species located in sites hundreds of miles apart. Because both species emerge from their burrows at the same time in the spring, that meant that the photographing would take two springs.

Caulfield then sought the expertise of researchers who were out in the field studying prairie dogs. She spent several days at a site in Utah to determine if she could get the shots she needed. At that point she put together a proposal for a photographic essay on prairie dogs and pitched it to major magazine editors. When one of them offered her a contract for the project, she went ahead with her field preparations. Only after many months of research and preparation, thousands of miles of driving across the West making arrangements, and two springs' worth of shooting did she get the pictures she was after.

Peggy and Erwin Bauer's work with ruffed grouse is a prime example of how preparation and luck work together. During one of

their many hikes into the Teton Mountains near their home, they heard the drumming of a ruffed grouse. The male grouse produce this distinctive sound by the beating of their wings in an annual ritual to attract females. The Bauers were able to find the grouse and the fallen Douglas fir trunk on which he was drumming. They made note of the location of the log for a later time.

From their observations and other sources, the Bauers calculated the average May day on which the drumming activity of grouse above 7,500 feet (2,290 meters) in elevation was at its peak. Early on this day, they returned to the drumming location. Since this was in a section of mountains that attracted many hikers, they figured the grouse would be used to the presence of humans and so they set up their cloth blind only 20 feet (6 meters) from the drumming log.

As they waited in the blind, a beam of sunlight lit up the center of the fallen fir log. At that moment, the grouse arrived and began strutting and beating its wings in that spotlighted portion. The result was a beautiful series of shots of a grouse drumming. While the light shaft and the grouse's timing were strokes of luck, only the Bauers' preparation and expertise allowed them to be in position to take advantage of it.

PREVOUS PAGES Amos Nachoum relied on his considerable diving skills to capture a humpback whale with calf in the deep. ABOVE Lots of planning and hard work enabled Pat Caulfield to get this photo of a prairie dog carrying nesting material to its burrow.

The Code of the Wildlife Photographer

In 1967, *Life* magazine showed one of the most stunning series of wildlife photographs ever produced. The camera captured a close-up view of a baboon fighting for its life against a leopard, followed by the leopard making the kill. A nature photographer had apparently pulled back nature's secretive curtain to show the raw

struggle for survival in its most savage form. But actually, the photographer did not record a natural event at all; instead, he staged a brutal spectacle. The animals were not discovered in the wild; they were placed together in a small enclosed area. The leopard was starved so that it

Tiger in the wild? Not really. This tiger was shot before a movie backdrop.

67

would be certain to attack the baboon immediately. Several baboons were thrown into the pen and killed by the leopard before the photographer got the shots he wanted.

Unnatural Nature Shots

The incident highlights a controversy that has plagued wildlife photography for half a century. In the 1950s, the Disney company produced a number of popular nature films, such as *The Living Desert*. Reports later surfaced that the film used trained, tame animals posing as wild creatures. A wildcat perched dramatically on a saguaro cactus was placed there by its handlers.

The debate over what is natural, honest, and proper in wildlife photography has grown more heated over the past several decades. Many of the beautiful wildlife shots that decorate calendars, atlases, books, and fill television airtime have little to do with the actual wilderness. The films and photographs of predators stalking and killing prey often take place in large compounds made to look like a natural environment. Photographs of rarely seen and endangered species are usually taken in zoos. In many cases, readers and viewers are led to believe the photographs are of actual wild animals. A 1994 photograph of a tiger on the cover of *Time* magazine included no mention of the fact that it was taken at the Minnesota Zoo. Dramatic shots of smallmouth bass leaping high out of the water have been staged using a water cannon to shoot the fish out of the water.

Computer Imaging

Modern computer programs have further muddied the waters as to what is real and what is fake in wildlife photography. With a click of a mouse, people who know nothing about nature can create stunning images that expert photographers could not hope to duplicate

in a lifetime. They can erase bars and concrete barriers from zoo photographs. They can add detail to sharpen blurred images or remove shadows. Digital technology allows computer experts to take animals from one photograph and place them in a different setting. The technology is so advanced that even experts often cannot tell if a photograph has been doctored.

Seattle photographer Art Wolfe used a computer to enhance images of about a third of the ninety-eight photographs he used in a book called *Migrations*. He has used computers to place a koala in a picturesque setting in Australia, even though no koalas live anywhere near the scene displayed.

Why the Artificial Route?

The difficulty and expense of getting certain wildlife photographs prompts photographers to stage photographs. Demand for unique and exciting wildlife photos is high. Editors in charge of getting those photographs have limited budgets. They can save a great deal of money by buying staged shots of captive animals, especially rare ones, rather than paying for a photographer to spend weeks in

Using a computer, Tim Fitzharris put together two shots of flamingos to get this perfectly balanced image.

the wild. Because editors demand high quality, they may be more likely to accept a crystal clear shot of an animal taken in a zoo than a blurred one of the animal in the wild. Their requests for spectacular shots of animals doing unusual things can often be fulfilled only by staging the shots.

"A big problem we see is an editor who says, 'I want this kind of a picture,' and then the word gets out," says Chuck Jonkel of the Wildlife Film Festival.

Joe McDonald argues that staging shots is the only practical way to obtain good photographs of North American predators such as cougars. The chances of finding one in the wild are "abysmally slim," he says. "Most American predators are uncommon or rare, and nocturnal or very shy."

Daniel J. Cox works with a friend in Montana who raises and trains performing animals. Cox creates enclosed natural settings for these animals and then photographs them. He argues that his methods give people access to samples of wild animal behavior that they otherwise would never have. Referring to his photographs of the birth of a mountain lion, he says, "I couldn't have gotten these shots any other way. I was right there, two feet away during his birth."

How do you catch an elusive wolf in the wild? Joel Sartore used bait.

No Apologies

Marty Stouffer, creator of the popular television nature series *Wild America*, makes no apologies for the fact that his series includes staged scenes. "These recreations depict authentic animal behavior in the wild and I'm comfortable with that," he says.

Those who stage their photo shoots claim that few wildlife photographers take pictures without interfering in some way with their subjects. For example, the technique of luring animals in view with bait or decoys involves human interference. Furthermore, staged photography of captive endangered animals keeps such fragile species safe from the hordes of photographers who might otherwise be hounding them.

Those who use computers to create photos justify their work in two ways.

Some, like Art Wolfe, draw a line between art and wildlife photography. Wolfe views his work as an artistic expression that is not intended to be taken as science. "We led the way in a beautiful new technology and I'm proud of that," he says. He views the complaints about computer enhancement as a "hysterical" reaction.

Tim Fitzharris, whose shots were selected for the cover of *Audubon* magazine four times in one year, argues that all cameras present an incomplete perspective of what they see. Lighting and motion problems can sometimes cause a photograph to present a distorted picture of reality. Fitzharris believes that, in some cases, digitally altering pictures can actually give a more accurate view of what nature really looks like.

The Public Trust

Many of the top wildlife photographers insist staged photographs and computer doctoring is wrong. Their primary argument is that these things tend to present a false view of the natural world. In one blatant example, a photographer spray painted the feet of common ferrets so that he could pass them off in his pictures as rare black-footed ferrets. A 1958 film called *White Wilderness* was another classic case of a staged film shoot misleading the public. The producers gathered over a thousand lemmings and drove them over a cliff for the cameras to record. This was supposed to depict the common lemming habit of committing mass suicide. The problem is that such behavior among lemmings is a myth.

National Geographic editor Bill Albin believes that computerized imaging is just a fancier way of promoting distortions and outright falsehoods about nature. "Technology is not taking us closer to reality but further from it," he says. Wildlife photographers are concerned that such false representations threaten to ruin their craft because, as Michael Nichols says, "To me, the public's trust is the most important thing we have."

For people like Tom Mangelson, the biggest problem with staged shoots, and zoo and game farm photos, is that they are the easy way out. Mangelson refuses to take any wildlife photos unless they are actually wild animals in their natural settings. He believes that those who take shortcuts in photographing wildlife cannot possibly gain the knowledge necessary to truly understand the animals and their habitat.

Respect for Nature

For Mangelson and others, the issue is a simple matter of respect for the natural world. This respect is at the heart of the code of behavior that most professional wildlife photographers follow with a passion. They see themselves not as exploiters or even observers

Decidedly unnatural, these tourists pursue a cheetah in one of Africa's wildlife parks.

of nature. Rather, each are what Jack Swedberg calls a "bridge" to nature. Their job is to spread the tremendous appreciation they have gained for the creatures of the wild to as many people as possible. The vast majority of wildlife photographers are actively involved in educating the public about wildlife. They are among the world's most passionate advocates of conservation measures to save what is left of the wild and to protect animals.

This attitude governs their approach to shooting wildlife with the camera. They cringe at the novice photographers who camp near African water holes, disturbing the animals with their presence. They fume at the amateur tourists who are so intent on taking their own photographs of a cheetah that they follow the graceful animals wherever they go. This harassment has forced some cheetahs—who normally hunt during the morning or late afternoon—into hunting at night, when they are less likely to be successful, thus endangering their survival.

For the responsible wildlife photographer, concern for the well-being of their subjects always comes first. "A shot should never take precedence over a subject's welfare," says Joe McDonald. For example, although a photographer may get a great shot of a nest by enticing a mother bird to leave the nest, he or she should first consider what that brief absence may do to the eggs or the babies. The best photographers will abandon a project and swallow the cost rather than put a subject at risk.

"When a wild animal accepts me into his or her world, I regard it as a privilege," says Frans Lanting. For the true professional wildlife photographer, earning that privilege is far more important than getting the picture.

For Frans Lanting, getting this engaging shot of a giant panda nibbling bamboo was its own reward.

Do you want to learn more about wildlife photography, or how you might become a wildlife photographer? Here are some ideas.

Join a Photography Club

Many schools and communities have photography clubs that you can join. Often these provide access to photographic facilities and darkrooms.

Take a Photography Course

Many schools and community colleges offer photography courses for beginners. Some photo shops, photo equipment manufacturers, and even professional photographers also offer occasional workshops or classes.

Practice, Practice, Practice

Practice taking photographs of animals in your backyard, park, recreation area, or zoo. Show them to others and get feedback as to how to improve. You might also enter your best shots in photo contests and see how you do. Many newspapers, magazines, photo clubs, and other organizations run photo contests.

Visit a Museum or Photo Gallery

Many museums and art galleries hold exhibitions of prominent photographers' works. A few specialize in photography, or have permanent collections on display.

Consult a Photographic Society or Other Organization

There are a number of photographic societies, associations, and organizations that publish useful information for photographers. Many of these offer forums, encourage youth participation, and have Web sites with links to other organizations and resources. Here are a few:

The Photographic Society of America
www.psa-photo.org

Society for Photographic Education
www.ppa-world.org

The Royal Photographic Society
www.rps.org

Join a Nature or Wildlife Conservation Group

Before you can become a good wildlife photographer, you must understand the ways of wildlife. Joining a nature or wildlife conservation group such as the National Audubon Society can help you on your way.

Read a Book or Magazine

There are numerous books with information of interest to the wildlife photographer (see *Further Reading*, page 77). In addition, wildlife and photography magazines of interest to the wildlife photographer abound. Check your local library, or an online library, for ideas.

Bauer, Peggy, and Erwin Bauer. *Wildlife Adventures With a Camera.* New York: Harry N. Abrams, 1984.

Bush, Vanessa. "Close Encounters." *Life*, October 1997.

Caulfield, Pat. *Photographing Wildlife.* New York: Amphoto, 1988.

Chapman, Wendell, and Lucie Chapman. "Lords of the Rockies." *National Geographic*, July 1939.

Cox, Daniel J. "Family Cat." *Life*, February 1999.

Finkel, Michael. "Scene Stealer." *National Wildlife*, October 1997.

Hile, Kevin S., ed. *Something About the Author*, Vol. 87. Detroit: Gale Research, 1996.

Lasky, Katherine. *Think Like an Eagle: At Work With a Wildlife Photographer.* Boston: Little, Brown & Company, 1992.

Lemmo, Gerry. "Mysterious Marten." *New York State Conservationist*, February 1999.

McDonald, Joe. *Designing Wildlife Photographs.* New York: Amphoto, 1994.

McKibben, Bill. "Curbing Nature's Paparazzi." *Harper's*, November 1997.

Rexer, Lyle. "Defenders of a Kingdom Long Swept Aside." *New York Times*, February 2, 1997.

Satchell, Michael. "Antarctica and the Polar Bear." *U.S. News & World Report*, January 12, 1998.

Shaw, John. *The Nature Photographer's Complete Guide to Professional Field Techniques.* New York: American Photographic Books, 1984.

Skinner, Peter. "Frans Lanting." *Peterson Photographic*, June 1997.

Taliaferro, Linda. "Shooting Monkeys Through Cameras." *New York Times*, December 8, 1996.

Truslow, Frederick Kent. "Businessman in the Bush." *National Geographic*, May 1970.

Van Lawick, Hugo. *Savage Paradise.* New York: Morrow, 1977.

Ward, Logan. "Close Calls." *American Photography*, May 1999.

Wexler, Mark. "Seeing Eye to Eye With Wildlife." *National Wildlife*, August 1998.

Ziesler, Gunter, and Angelika Hofer. *Safari.* New York: Facts On File, 1984.

CREDITS

To Norm and Sharla

Designed by Carolyn Eckert

Front and back cover photographs courtesy of © Frans Lanting/Minden Pictures

Photographs courtesy of © Minden Pictures/Jim Brandenburg: pp. 1, 23, 27; © Gunter Ziesler/Peter Arnold, Inc.: pp. 2-3; © Thomas D. Mangelsen/Images of Nature: pp. 4-5, 46-47, 49; © Joe McDonald: p. 6; © Erwin & Peggy Bauer: pp. 10, 24; © Frank & John Craighead/NGS Image Collection: p. 13; © J. E. Swedberg: pp. 16-17, 19, 31, 32, 38-39; © F. Truslow/VIREO: p. 28; © Patricia Caulfield: pp. 37, 65; © Frans Lanting/Minden Pictures: pp. 41, 74; © Rosa Maria Ruiz/NGS Image Collection: p. 43; © Peter Arnold, Inc./Nicole Duplaix: pp. 50-51; © Peter Arnold, Inc./Galen Rowell: p. 55; © Stephen Durst/Minden Pictures: p. 58; © TSM/1998 Amos Nachoum: pp. 62-63; Culver Pictures, Inc.: pp. 66-67; © Tim Fitzharris/Minden Pictures: p. 69; www.Joel Sartore.com: p. 70; © Gerry Ellis/Minden Pictures: p. 73.

The Library of Congress Control Number: 00-045089
ISBN 0-7613-1551-9 (lib. bdg.)

Published by The Millbrook Press, Inc.
2 Old New Milford Road
Brookfield, Connecticut 06804
www.millbrookpress.com

Copyright © 2001 by Nathan Aaseng
All rights reserved.
Printed in Hong Kong
5 4 3 2 1